Message Sent

Message Sent

THE FEEDBACK TEACHERS HAVE BEEN ASKING FOR FROM AN ADMINISTRATIVE PERSPECTIVE

Kamilah D. Holden

Printed in the United States of America

ISBN-13: 9781523384563
ISBN-10: 1523384565
Library of Congress Control Number: 2016900659
CreateSpace Independent Publishing Platform
North Charleston, South Carolina

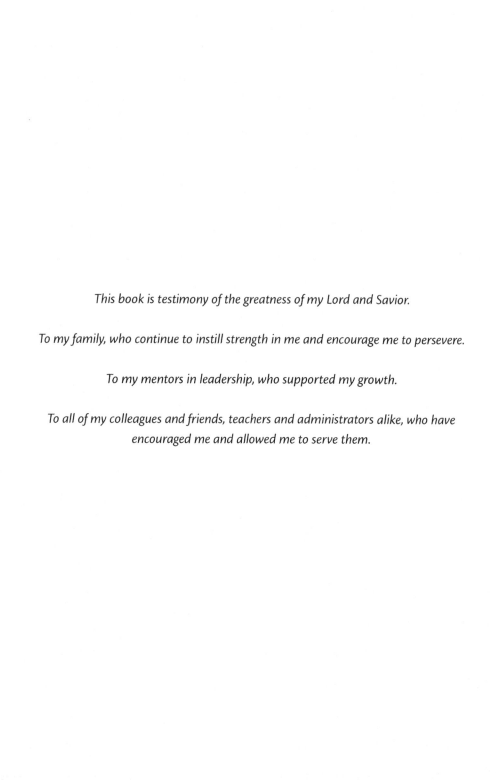

This book is testimony of the greatness of my Lord and Savior.

To my family, who continue to instill strength in me and encourage me to persevere.

To my mentors in leadership, who supported my growth.

To all of my colleagues and friends, teachers and administrators alike, who have encouraged me and allowed me to serve them.

Preface

————

THIS BOOK IS DEDICATED TO the many educators who are in need of a practical reference for providing or understanding feedback on classroom instruction. I have spent over a decade in the educational field as a teacher, instructional coach, assistant principal, and principal in some of the largest school districts in the United States. I have also served with the Florida Department of Education, supporting districts and school-based leadership teams in developing school-wide systems for school-improvement efforts. All of these experiences led me to writing this book.

One of the most important formulas in improving schools is rooted in the feedback provided to teachers on their instructional practices in the classroom. The classroom is where it all happens.

Feedback needs to provide information specifically relating to the task or process of learning that fills a gap between what is understood and what is aimed to be understood.

Sadler (as cited in Hattie & Timperley, 2007, p. 82)

It is my belief that teachers want to do their best in the classroom; however, they may not know how. I believe that administrators want to provide meaningful feedback to teachers; however, they may not know how. The school-based administrative role is constantly evolving into instructional leader versus building administrator or administrator over discipline. Being knowledgeable about content and best practices makes an administrator valuable. With very elaborate evaluation systems focused on instructional strategies and best practices, and with performance pay and instructional targets tied to standards, it is important for all stakeholders to have an understanding of how to provide meaningful feedback and support.

> *Providing feedback to teachers about the results of their observations and helping them reflect on this feedback in productive ways provides the bridge between knowledge about what matters for students and changes in teachers' actual practice.*

> **(Stuhlman, Hamre, Downer, & Pianta, n.d., p. 3)**

Though not the only factor, feedback plays a vital role in improving instruction and, ultimately, student achievement. My hope is that school-based leadership teams and teachers will engage in this book side by side in support of other efforts such as professional development and instructional coaching support. These support efforts, aligned with continuous feedback on instructional practices, can tremendously impact teacher performance.

> *Professional development is most effective when it is constructed around helping teachers make improvements in areas of their job that really matter for students, when those areas targeted for observation and improvement are clearly defined, and when all participants agree that the targets of the observation are valid goals to work towards.*

> **(Stuhlman et al., n.d., p. 3)**

Message Sent is a compilation that targets several instructional and high-yield strategies—as constructive and actionable feedback to teachers on practices observed during instruction—through an administrative lens. As a resource to bridge the gap between teachers and administrators, it will give educational teams a better understanding, through real-time scenarios and questioning, of the "message sent" during classroom observations.

> *Talented people depend on others for honest assessments of their work in determining what to do better. Without feedback about their performance, they have a hard time figuring out how to improve. With constructive feedback, they can learn sooner and with much greater specificity.*

(Cannon & Witherspoon, 2005, p. 121)

The compilation is divided into four sections: instructional delivery, grouping, student tasks, and classroom management with student engagement. Following each of the nineteen scenarios is the "Message Sent," which is meant to depict what the administrator is inferring. The "Administration Might Ask" questions will support administrators in probing teachers to develop their own conclusions as to their own effectiveness. The "Constructive Feedback" serves as specific, actionable guidance, and the "Example-in-Practice Scenario" represents real-time best-case practices.

Let's all join in the journey toward continuous improvement.

Thank you!

Table of Contents

I. Instructional Delivery

___

———

To prepare the students for the day's instruction, they should enter the classroom and begin with a morning or class routine.
Your first priority when class begins is not to take the roll; it is to get the students to work. An assignment must be available, and the students must know the procedure for getting to work immediately.

(Wong & Wong, 2000)

———

SCENARIO 1

Beginning Class Routine

———

THE BELL HAS RUNG, AND some students are still walking into the classroom. Some are standing around talking, and there has been no direction or redirection by the teacher for instruction to start.

MESSAGE SENT:
The teacher has not established a routine for instruction to start at the bell, and therefore instructional minutes are not being used effectively.

ADMINISTRATION MIGHT ASK:
What is the expectation of the students as they enter the classroom?

CONSTRUCTIVE FEEDBACK:
Establish a routine of instruction at the bell in which students are empowered as they enter the classroom by knowing which task they should be engaged in as the bell rings (for instance, bell work, bell ringer). Establish and consistently state the procedures students should be following upon entering the classroom—for example, sharpen pencils, take out paper, and get started on bell work. Monitor students, and redirect those not following procedures.

EXAMPLE-IN-PRACTICE SCENARIO:

As students enter Mr. Jackson's class, the procedure is for them to sit down and pull out their materials while looking at the board for the short assignment they are to complete. The assignment may be different from day to day but is found in the same spot every day. Mr. Jackson is consistently reminding students of the procedure as they enter until all students have started on the assignment. He consistently acknowledges students with positive praise for following the procedure.

Pacing the lesson means balancing content delivery, practice time, and checks for understanding. If the opening of the lesson lasts 15 minutes, less time is available for the main focus and practice that are necessary to improve skills. The same is true if the main portion of the lesson lasts 45 minutes of a 50 minute period. Students will not have time to review and apply their learning or practice independently before they leave the classroom with homework that they may not understand.

(Cunningham, 2009, p. 111)

SCENARIO 2

Lesson Pacing

———

TWENTY-FIVE MINUTES INTO A CLASS period, students are still engaged in the same assignment they were engaged in at the beginning bell.

MESSAGE SENT:
The teacher has not planned for the effective use of time during the period.

ADMINISTRATION MIGHT ASK:
How are you using bell work for instruction, and how much time are you allotting for bell work in your lesson plan?

CONSTRUCTIVE FEEDBACK:
During the planning process, plan within an instructional framework that defines the amount of time to be spent in the class period on bell work, whole-group instruction, guided and independent practice, and whole-group wrap-up. Bell work is not meant to be used as the assignment of the day. Bell work is meant to be used to activate prior knowledge, preview the lesson, reinforce previous content, formatively assess student knowledge, and so forth. Typically this portion of the instruction should span no more than five to ten minutes of the instructional day. This means that the task required of the students should be doable within that time frame, including assessment, reflection, discussion, or review of the task.

EXAMPLE-IN-PRACTICE SCENARIO:

Mr. Jackson's routine of preparedness at the bell includes setting a timer for five minutes to support lesson pacing. Students generally have tasks that can be completed within that time frame; however, if his observations of student responses reveal the need for an extra minute, he has allotted time in his lesson plan for this adjustment before reviewing responses. Should students finish earlier, he then makes the adjustment to start his review earlier than intended. Bell work may last about five to seven minutes but not more than ten minutes. The rest of his instructional minutes are strategically allocated to ensure that students engage in explicit instruction, guided and independent practice, and whole-group wrap-up.

———

Structured teaching requires that teachers know their students and content well, that they regularly assess students' understanding of the content, and that they purposefully plan interrelated lessons that transfer responsibility from the teacher to the student. Gradual release of responsibility is the theory that guides this type of teaching.

(Fisher & Frey, 2013, pp. 16–17)

———

SCENARIO 3

Gradual Release

———

THE CLASS HAS JUST STARTED a new lesson. After the teacher lectures and models a skill, the students are released to independent practice. Most students are confused and cannot work independently without teacher support.

MESSAGE SENT:

There is a need for guided practice and checks for understanding in whole group before the release to independent practice.

ADMINISTRATION MIGHT ASK:

Which strategies can you implement that will help you gauge student understanding of the concepts in whole group and inform their readiness to move forward?

Did students have adequate time to practice during whole group before moving into independent practice?

CONSTRUCTIVE FEEDBACK:

Incorporate the gradual release model into your lesson delivery. The teacher will model the skill, guide students in the practice of the skill, and then allow time for students to collaborate and support one another, while the teacher facilitates, before practicing independently. This model will ensure an adequate amount of practice and support before releasing to independent practice.

EXAMPLE-IN-PRACTICE SCENARIO:

Mr. Jackson is delivering a math lesson. He first models a problem while thinking aloud. The students are simply observing and listening. Mr. Jackson then invites the group to support him in answering a number of problems while students take notes and engage in group discussion around the concepts. He consistently seeks the understanding of the group through planned questioning and monitoring of their anecdotal thoughts. He then releases them to work collaboratively with one another for peer support and practice, using various cooperative structures to ensure that students challenge one another in thought. During this time, the tasks are scaffolded to increase in cognitive demand. If Mr. Jackson determines that the students need more guidance than facilitation, he pulls them back to whole group to engage further into guided practice. They may move from modeling, to guided, and back to collaboration various times before graduating to independent practice.

The degree of improvement resulting from increases in both higher cognitive questions and wait-time is greater than an increase in either of these variables by itself.

Redirection and probing are positively related to achievement when they are explicitly focused, e.g., on the clarity, accuracy, plausibility, etc. of student responses.

(Cotton, 1989, pp. 23–24)

SCENARIO 4

Questioning

———

THE TEACHER IS ASKING AND answering the majority of questions posed to students.

MESSAGE SENT:

The students have not had the opportunity to demonstrate their understanding of the topics being addressed, and the teacher is not authentically seeking student understanding.

ADMINISTRATION MIGHT ASK:

How do you know that students comprehend the topic or concept if, during questioning, you do not authentically elicit and expect a response?

CONSTRUCTIVE FEEDBACK:

When posing questions to students, use strategies to support the provision of wait time. Questions should be strategically planned and purposeful, and so should the answers you are seeking. Use probing strategies to challenge and encourage students toward acceptable responses. Teacher answers or elaborations should be followed by student thinking and understanding through paraphrasing strategies, text evidences, and examples supporting understandings or through student elaborations of the concepts.

EXAMPLE-IN-PRACTICE SCENARIO:

Mr. Jackson is explicitly instructing during a whole-group lesson. At strategic points in his lesson, he stops to pose questions to the students to either check their understanding or to probe extended thinking. As he poses questions, it is habit for him to wait ten seconds before asking another question. If no students respond, he may ask them to turn and talk to a partner before posing that question again. If a question is posed to a single student who cannot answer, he may ask that student to turn and talk to a partner, think about the answer for a minute, or review his or her notes while he moves on to another student. He always returns to the initial student afterward. If students continue to struggle, he offers his thoughts and asks them to reexamine and share their understanding with text evidence or examples.

Unpacking the standards and using them to develop learning goals will help focus your instructional planning. Not only will it help you determine what exactly students should learn, it will help you select learning activities that are well-matched to the learning goals and to students' individual needs.

(Jackson, 2009, p. 60)

SCENARIO 5

Standards-Driven Lessons

———

THE STANDARD BEING ADDRESSED IN the instruction is adding and subtracting two- and three-digit numbers. The lesson only addresses one- and two-digit numbers with no anticipation within the lesson plan reflecting three-digit numbers.

MESSAGE SENT:
The lesson was not planned to address all parts (full intent) of the standard.

ADMINISTRATION MIGHT ASK:
In order to address the full intent of the standard, will your lesson address opportunities for students to add and subtract three-digit numbers?

CONSTRUCTIVE FEEDBACK:
Before planning your lessons, deconstruct the standards by breaking them down to define specific targets to be mastered. Then reconstruct those targets into procedural or declarative objectives that will guide the planning of your daily lessons. As the lesson is scaffolded to meet the needs of the students, be sure to include explicit instruction and activities that will allow students mastery at the full intent of the standard.

EXAMPLE-IN-PRACTICE SCENARIO:

Mr. Jackson leads collaborative planning weekly at JFK School. The objective of the planning is for the teachers of the same content and grade to plan common lessons. Mr. Jackson knows that in order for the team to plan common lessons, they have to develop a common understanding of what the standard is asking. In order to achieve this goal, planning starts with a collaborative deconstruction of the standard. Using the deconstructed targets, the team then creates common daily objectives and assessment tasks measuring those objectives. By following this structure, Mr. Jackson ensures that the teachers have common starting and ending goals. Lastly, the team, individually or collaboratively, creates or aligns assignments/activities to carry out the objectives. If done so individually, the product is shared and analyzed by the group.

After the lessons are taught and assessed, individual teacher responsibility is to analyze the assessment data, reflect on successes and gaps in the lesson, and identify concepts needing remediation. The group allocates a little time in the following planning session to share results and resources for remediation.

_____

Consider a few ready-made educational resources with which you are familiar. What potential can you see for:

* *Using them selectively, omitting some of the material?*

* *Adaption: extending the material of using it more fully?*

* *Supplementation: bringing in fresh material to use in conjunction with the original resource?*

* *Radically changing the resource, for example, by replacing parts of it?*

(Haynes, 2010, p. 89)

_____

SCENARIO 6

Teaching Religiously from the Book

———

THE TEACHER IS TEACHING PAGE for page from a textbook. Students are minimally engaged and performing poorly on common assessments.

MESSAGE SENT:

The textbook is being used as the curriculum for the class and not as a resource to support the curriculum.

ADMINISTRATION MIGHT ASK:

Are there other resources that can be used in addition to the textbook to ensure that your lessons are engaging and support the full intent of the standard being addressed?

CONSTRUCTIVE FEEDBACK:

Our curriculum outlines standards that should be addressed in order for students to reach mastery of the course outcomes. The textbook is a resource that supports the curriculum and should be supplemented when it does not address the full intent of the standards or does not offer engaging and differentiated opportunities for students to conceptually grasp the concepts.

EXAMPLE-IN-PRACTICE SCENARIO:

When planning lessons, Mr. Jackson starts with deconstructing the standard and reviewing test-item specifications to grasp and understand the standard. He then seeks out differentiated activities from many sources that will meet the intent of the standard and foster student engagement. He uses the textbook along with various resources found on the Internet or in other texts as well as those he creates.

———

A factor that appears to make the difference lies in the ability of district and building administrators and teachers to make data-driven decisions that result in changes to instruction. Most commonly, these instructional changes are evidenced in the identification of students who are lagging behind.

(James-Ward, Fisher, & Frey, 2013, p. 95)

———

SCENARIO 7

Progress Monitoring

———

STUDENTS ARE GIVEN ASSESSMENTS AFTER every lesson, which the teacher grades and then returns. Meanwhile, the teacher has moved on to the next lesson, never addressing the assessment or concepts in the assessment again.

MESSAGE SENT:

All students have met proficiency on the concepts or benchmarks addressed in the lesson.

ADMINISTRATION MIGHT ASK:

What evidence do you have that supports all students meeting mastery of the benchmarks addressed by the lesson being assessed? If none, how can you adjust your instruction for reteaching of the previous lesson while moving forward in the current lesson?

CONSTRUCTIVE FEEDBACK:

After analyzing the data collected from the assessment, build in opportunities for reteaching or enrichment. You will want to differentiate your instruction to meet the individual needs of the students based on the data. This could happen in small-group settings during class, or students can be assigned mini lessons to work on out of classroom settings. All opportunities should be monitored by the teacher, ending in reassessment of the concepts.

EXAMPLE-IN-PRACTICE SCENARIO:

Mr. Jackson is passing back an assessment to his students and asks them to highlight those items they had gotten wrong. He then begins to explain to the students that they as a class, during bell work, will be revisiting over the next week a few concepts everyone struggled with, and he has them circle the questions that correspond to those concepts. He then passes out a reteaching guide that he calls "Mastering the Odds," with mini lessons that should be completed if students highlighted a specific group of questions. The mini lessons may contain reteaching videos or simulations for students to see the content in different ways. The students retest after completing the lessons, continuing this cycle until mastery is met. All future assessments contain questions from previous retaught standards to monitor retention of the concepts.

II. Grouping

_____

———

Guided instruction is dependent on insight into students' learning status; it's how teachers form groups and how they decide what to teach to these groups.

(Fisher & Frey, 2013, p. 127)

———

SCENARIO 8

Teacher-Led Small Group

AS THE TEACHER IS FORMATIVELY questioning the class during guided practice, there are a few students who are consistently answering incorrectly; however, all students transitioned to the next phase of the lesson.

MESSAGE SENT:

The students are moving forward with gaps in their understanding.

ADMINISTRATION MIGHT ASK:

How can you support the students who are not ready to move on while the others who *are* ready continue?

CONSTRUCTIVE FEEDBACK:

Plan for teacher-led small-group instruction to take place in the day to support anticipated points of struggle in the lesson. This way students do not move forward unengaged with gaps in their learning.

EXAMPLE-IN-PRACTICE SCENARIO:

When planning his lessons, Mr. Jackson plans formative questions to help him gauge student thinking and understanding during guided instruction. Students who struggle with the questions and the content are asked to join a planned small group with him before moving forward in the lesson. Students who are ready to move forward engage in collaborative planned practice.

———

Grouping is both highly flexible and fluid. Student groupings are responsive to both student needs and content goals, and tasks within groups are designed to draw on the strengths of the individuals in those groups.

(Tomlinson, 2014, p. 23)

———

SCENARIO 9

Grouping Students/DI

———

STUDENTS ARE SEATED IN ROWS daily and have minimal opportunities to collaborate with other students in the class about the lessons.

MESSAGE SENT:

Students do not have many opportunities to participate in authentic collaborative conversations, in which they are able to support and challenge one another and engage with practices aligned to shifts in the common core standards.

ADMINISTRATION MIGHT ASK:

How might you adjust the orientation of your classroom to encourage student collaboration and practices aligned with shifts in the common core standards?

CONSTRUCTIVE FEEDBACK:

Students should be grouped to encourage collaboration, allowing them to learn from one another's thinking and reasoning. Students can be grouped in various ways using quantitative and/or qualitative data. During whole-group instruction, students can be heterogeneously grouped with differing levels of ability to support one another. You will want to take qualitative measures into account as well, such as behavioral factors. When breaking them into small groups, you will want your student arrangement to support differentiated tasks when student performance data shows a need. Groups can be homogenous (all students at the same level relative to a specific data point) or heterogeneous. The activities in the various groups should support the needs of individual students and should be preplanned.

EXAMPLE-IN-PRACTICE SCENARIO:

At the start of his unit, Mr. Jackson provided a pretest so that he can group his students for whole-group instruction. He often groups them in a heterogeneous manner for whole-group and guided practice so that the students are able to support one another. Before students are released to collaborative practice, he provides a formative assessment—which guides the regrouping of students to support gaps in understanding—in a small-group setting. He often has a group supporting foundational skills, which is teacher led; a technology group for those needing a little less guided support; and an enrichment group for those who are ready to be challenged. In the technology group, students are on various guided programs that support the skills for which they are in need of support based on the assessment data. Each of his small-group stations is aligned to a standards-driven objective, and the number and content of the groups depend on the standard demands. He incorporates collaborative structures into group instructions to ensure maximum engagement from all students.

At the day's end, Mr. Jackson invites students back to whole group to revisit key concepts, which they should have now mastered, in preparation for further independent practice at home.

Never choose an outcome one student could do alone. In addition, fre-
quently reinforce the idea that the purpose of the team is to make sure
that all members are learning, not just to get the right answers or com-
plete the project.

(Slavin, 2014, p. 24)

SCENARIO 10

Cooperative Structures

———

STUDENTS ARE WORKING IN GROUPS; however, there are one or two students doing all of the work while the other students are copying or doing nothing at all.

MESSAGE SENT:

The students who are copying or not working are not learning. The teacher has not established a structure or incorporated strategies to encourage collaboration in groups.

ADMINISTRATION MIGHT ASK:

What structures can you incorporate into the groups to support all students with participation and engagement in the learning?

CONSTRUCTIVE FEEDBACK:

When allowing group activities, incorporate structures that will encourage all students to take part and have accountability in the learning. For example, establish group roles that are significant and relative to the task. Design tasks that are dependent upon whole-group participation. Provide conversation starters or question stems that the students must ask one another. Put group performance accountability measures in place to support students holding one another accountable.

EXAMPLE-IN-PRACTICE SCENARIO:

During a lab in Mr. Jackson's science block, there are four important factors that need consistent attention: time measurement, accuracy of data collection, precision in moving through procedure, and carrying out a simulation. In Mr. Jackson's class, everyone is a recorder, so based on the task, he splits the class into groups of three. The roles assigned include the measureator (person in charge of time measurement throughout the lab), precisionator (person in charge of ensuring that the procedure was carried out with precision), and simulator (person in charge of carrying out the simulation). Everyone carries out the role of accurator, ensuring accuracy of data collection. It is a practice of his to model tasks before releasing them to the students so he can simulate each person's role in the process. As the students carry out the lab, he observes, probes students' thinking, and refocuses any student not performing the assigned roles.

III. Student Tasks

———

————

Working with the material should require students to stretch—to employ critical and creative thinking and their background knowledge to construct new meaning and acquire new skills.

(Jackson, 2011, p. 42)

————

SCENARIO 11

Rigorous Instruction

———

STUDENTS ARE COMPLETING A LAB in a science class by following the procedures step by step and recording information. They have already been instructed in class on the content of the lab and are already aware of the outcome. There is no evidence of questioning to probe student thinking beyond or at the level of what they are engaged in.

MESSAGE SENT:
The lab lacks rigor and does not allow opportunities for students to make connections to the content or to think beyond what has been explicitly addressed in the lesson.

ADMINISTRATION MIGHT ASK:
How might you modify this lab to include inquiry and opportunities for students to explore the content through the lab, clear up misconceptions in thinking, and make real-world connections?

CONSTRUCTIVE FEEDBACK:
Build rigor in your lessons through open-ended questioning and probing that encourages student exploration to find answers. Allow students to challenge and critique one another, presenting evidence to support their thinking. Use

resources such as depth-of-knowledge (DOK) questions and tasks that support standard complexity, common core mathematical practices, and reading shifts to guide the planning of your lessons.

EXAMPLE-IN-PRACTICE SCENARIO:

Mr. Jackson considers himself an old-school teacher; however, his administrators and peers consider him very innovative and engaging. His instruction in all subject areas always includes some form of inquiry. For example, when teaching a topic, he always begins with taking students through the actual scenario in a real-world experience without telling them what they are exploring in order to build background knowledge. As the students start formulating their own ideas and thinking about the topic, he begins to help them make connections relative to the concepts through strategic questioning and by probing their thinking. He then allows them to grapple with the content, making connections to the previous explorations and current vocabulary and further proving their thinking with text evidence supported by rich content resources. Finally, using those experiences, students are given opportunities to elaborate and extend their thinking in different contexts.

———

Research on notetaking indicates that taking notes in class and reviewing those notes (either in class or afterward) have a positive impact on student learning.

(DeZure, Kaplan, & Deerman, 2001, p. 1)

Classroom management comprises a plan—a set of procedures that structure the classroom so the students know what to do, how to do it, and when to do it in the classroom.

(Wong, Wong, Rogers, & Brooks, 2012, p. 61)

———

SCENARIO 12

Note-Taking Procedure

———

THE TEACHER IS LECTURING FROM the front of the classroom using a Power Point presentation. Some students are taking notes, and some are not.

MESSAGE SENT:

The teacher has not established a procedure for what students should be doing during the lecture (taking notes) or has not reiterated and monitored the expectation of the procedure established.

ADMINISTRATION MIGHT ASK:

How will students be able to reflect on or further engage with the information presented in the lecture if they are not taking notes?

CONSTRUCTIVE FEEDBACK:

Before beginning your lesson, establish the procedure (note taking) that students should follow during the lecture. Frequently scan the room and often become proximal to monitor that students are following the procedure and have an understanding of the content. Be sure to restate the procedure and ultimately provide consequences when students do not comply.

EXAMPLE-IN-PRACTICE SCENARIO:

Before Mr. Jackson began the guided notes section of his lesson, he informed the students that he would prompt them at specific points to take notes but that everyone should actively participate in discussion until that time. As Mr. Jackson prompts for note taking during the lesson, he is walking around the class to ensure that students are taking notes and have an understanding of what they are writing and why they are writing it. He does so by asking clarifying and reflective questions. If there are students who do not begin writing upon his prompt, he restates the procedure: "Everyone should be writing at this time." Mr. Jackson's students know that he will be walking around and asking questions, so they rarely need more than one additional prompt. They also know that he consistently references previous notes, which students are expected to revise or expand upon based on their most current thinking.

———

At its best, an interactive notebook provides a varied set of strategies to create a personal, organized, and documented learning record.

(Waldman & Crippen, 2009, p. 51)

———

SCENARIO 13

Interactive Notebook

———

The teacher is asking students to look back at notes that were provided in a previous lesson or is making statements starting, "Remember when we...?" Some students are pulling out balled-up and wrinkled papers from their book bags, and others do not have these papers at all. Some are flipping through pages in their notebooks, for they know it is there somewhere.

Message Sent:

There is no organized method of storing notes or assignments for students to later reflect upon or study.

Administration Might Ask:

How can you support students in organizing their notes and assignments so that they are able to reference them, reflect on them, examine errors, and revise their thinking in current and upcoming lessons?

Constructive Feedback:

Put a notebook in place to help students organize notes within lessons, implementing page numbers and content sections to help them organize their thinking—for example, an interactive notebook that separately organizes student thinking and teacher-directed activities. This form of notebook encourages student reflection along with self-examination and revision of the student's own thinking and reasoning.

EXAMPLE-IN-PRACTICE SCENARIO:

Mr. Jackson has a table of contents posted in his classroom for all students to see. When the class is starting a new assignment, he adds the name of the assignment and the page it will be found on to that table of contents. This allows all students present and those absent to keep up with what has taken place in the daily lessons. Every assignment and activity has a page in the notebook; even those he collects and redistributes after grading are later glued or taped in. Graphic organizers, foldables, worksheets—everything goes in on assigned pages. During class discussions, he is able to ask students to turn to specific pages in the notebook to reflect on, examine, and sometimes revise past thinking and reasoning. To further support organization of thought, he always provides notes in some form of graphic organizers, which are helpful to all students, including ESE and ELL. In order to hold students accountable for the notebooks, every two weeks Mr. Jackson chooses a page range of assignments to grade or provide credit for. He also provides a notebook grade, which is determined by a rubric for upkeep of the notebook.

———

Rigorous learning materials alone do not guarantee that a lesson will be rigorous. If students are asked to interact with rigorous material in a simplistic or rote manner or if the learning activities around the material do not ask them to make their own meaning and practice rigorous thinking and problem-solving, the lesson will not be rigorous.

(Jackson, 2011, p. 58)

———

SCENARIO 14

Ineffective Use of Time: Copying

STUDENTS ARE COPYING LONG QUESTIONS before answering them, drawing pictures out of a book, or copying copious notes from the board.

MESSAGE SENT:
Students are engaged in busy work, and therefore instructional minutes are not being used effectively.

ADMINISTRATION MIGHT ASK:
How can you modify this lesson to reflect a more rigorous approach to using these resources?

Might you provide the questions or pictures to the students so that they spend more time reflecting, hypothesizing, interpreting, or demonstrating understanding of the concepts being addressed?

CONSTRUCTIVE FEEDBACK:
Every task provided to students should elicit cognitive engagement. Students should be provided with long questions, pictures out of books, and notes that they do not interact with. Instructional minutes should be spent answering the questions, interpreting or reflecting on pictures, and interacting with notes.

EXAMPLE-IN-PRACTICE SCENARIO:

Mr. Jackson often starts lessons with a cognitively demanding question that may include a lengthy question stem. It is imperative that students have the questions and answers as parts of their notes. Instead of asking the students to write the questions, Mr. Jackson provides the questions on quarter sheets of paper, which students attach in their notebooks, so that the time in class is spent answering and discussing the questions.

IV. Classroom Management and Student Engagement

Effective managers monitored their classroom regularly. They positioned themselves so that they could see all students and they continuously scanned the room to keep track of what was going on, no matter what else they were doing at the time.

Good & Brophy (as cited in Marzano, Gaddy, & Foseid, 2005, p. 84)

SCENARIO 15

Teaching from the Front of the Class

———

THE TEACHER HAS BEEN TEACHING an entire lesson from the front of the classroom with minimal student engagement.

MESSAGE SENT:

The teacher is not aware of what the students are actually engaged in, and student work is not being monitored.

ADMINISTRATION MIGHT ASK:

How do you know what students are doing or are engaged in if you are not proximal with them or scanning for and redirecting off-task behaviors?

CONSTRUCTIVE FEEDBACK:

When delivering instruction from the front of the classroom, be sure to consistently scan and periodically circulate around the room to monitor student work and engagement.

EXAMPLE-IN-PRACTICE SCENARIO:

When Mr. Jackson is delivering a Power Point presentation, he uses a clicker to navigate the slides so that he is able to remain proximal and monitor student engagement. This, in addition to questioning, allows him to gauge points at which he may need to adjust his instruction. In the absence of a clicker, he manually changes the slides; however, all conversations relevant to the slides take place as Mr. Jackson circulates around the room, moving back and forth from the board to annotate critical information. When performing demonstrations, he relies on consistent scanning and questioning to maintain engagement.

―――――

A teacher may expect that all students complete assignments and contrib-ute in class, but those expectations begin with early planning, continue with monitoring student performance, and then proceed with providing clear, concrete feedback to students.

(Stronge, Tucker, & Hindman, 2004, p. 202)

―――――

SCENARIO 16

Proximity and Monitoring

———

AS ADMINISTRATION MEMBERS ENTER THE classroom, the teacher is hastily getting up from his or her desk. Some students are engaged in the assignment; some are not. Some are much further along than others, and some have not started.

MESSAGE SENT:

The teacher has spent most of his or her time at the desk. Student tasks have not been monitored, feedback is not being provided, and instruction is not taking place.

ADMINISTRATION MIGHT ASK:

How do you know what your students are doing or if they are progressing on the assignment if you are not proximal and monitoring?

CONSTRUCTIVE FEEDBACK:

After releasing a task to students, remain proximal with them, consistently checking for understanding, providing feedback, and monitoring for on-task behaviors.

EXAMPLE-IN-PRACTICE SCENARIO:

As students are released to collaborative and ultimately independent practice, Mr. Jackson consistently walks around the room, probing student understanding, answering questions, providing feedback, and making certain that students are engaged in on-task behaviors. Any student not authentically engaged is redirected.

———

If students who think they have the answer are not permitted to verbalize their solution, the other students will continue trying to find the solution for themselves. (The person who thinks, learns.)

(Willis, 2006, p. 44)

———

SCENARIO 17

Eliciting Student Response

———

DURING WHOLE-GROUP INSTRUCTION, THE TEACHER is asking questions and eliciting group responses from students; however, there are one or two students answering every question.

MESSAGE SENT:

There are only one or two students engaged in the lesson and demonstrating understanding of the concepts. The teacher is not seeking—nor does he or she have a gauge on—the understanding of the group.

ADMINISTRATION MIGHT ASK:

How do you know the group is engaged and has an understanding of the concepts if only two students are responding to questioning?

CONSTRUCTIVE FEEDBACK:

When allowing group response, listen to responses while scanning the room and looking for students who are not responding. Revert to individual responses and wait-time strategies when engagement is not high among students. Use varying strategies to support randomization and methods of eliciting responses to increase engagement (for example, talking chips, random sticks, and white boards).

EXAMPLE-IN-PRACTICE SCENARIO:

Mr. Jackson has instructed his class to use white boards to respond to various questions. As he scans the room, he notices that there are various students not responding. Mr. Jackson says before his next question, "I want you all to turn to your partners and discuss the question first before responding on one white board for the group." He also prompts them to be ready to provide an explanation of the group's thinking. When Mr. Jackson views the boards this time around, he calls on those who had not been responding to share their groups' thinking. This allows him the opportunity to further probe the students' understanding and increase engagement.

———

When the teacher takes the time to teach a procedure carefully, it sends a message to students that this is important. Whenever a procedure has been taught, the teacher needs to monitor carefully. As soon as things begin to slip, stop and reteach.

(McLeod, Fisher, & Hoover, 2003, p. 92)

———

Call to Attention

———

THE MAJORITY OF STUDENTS IN the class are off task and not listening to the teacher as directions are provided for the upcoming assignment. Therefore, after being prompted to begin, half the students are stating that they don't understand what to do. As a result, the teacher is moving about the class, explaining the assignment to individual students.

MESSAGE SENT:

Students are not listening and are not being held accountable to any routine, procedure, or rule that should be followed while the teacher is instructing. Instructional minutes are lost while the students wait for the teacher to provide each of them with individual direction.

ADMINISTRATION MIGHT ASK:

Is there a routine or procedure established to encourage student engagement in on-task behaviors when receiving direction/instruction?

What strategies can you implement to gain the students' attention before providing direction/instruction?

CONSTRUCTIVE FEEDBACK:

When addressing or trying to regain attention of the whole class, use strategies such as a call to attention. Establish procedure defining what students should be doing as a result of the call. For example, as you count backward from five to zero, students should be finishing conversations and be engaged in active listening at zero. At zero, you will want to restate what it means to be actively listening (for example, all eyes on the teacher and all ears open, ready to listen and engage).

EXAMPLE-IN-PRACTICE SCENARIO:

Mr. Jackson has allowed the students some time to talk about a concept they are addressing in class. When time is up, Mr. Jackson starts a common phrase, "Today is a..." The students respond by saying, "Great day." He repeats the same phrase to ensure that everyone has responded as he monitors the response. He then begins to say, "If today is a great day, then we are actively listening, which means we are done talking, our ears are open, and all eyes are on me." He then addresses the class with the lesson. The "great day" phrase is often substituted for various motivational phrases to build confidence, motivation, and relationships with the students.

––––––

Teachers should respond to the minor behaviors before the behaviors become more severe.

(Martella, Nelson, & Marchand-Martella, 2011, p. 188)

A structured learning environment provides students with reasonable action alternatives; they are able to predict the consequences of their own behavior and receive feedback on inappropriate actions.

(Kunter, Baumert, & Köller, 2007, p. 496)

––––––

SCENARIO 19

Discipline Progression

———

STUDENTS ARE OFF TASK AND not following rules or procedures. The teacher redirects the students and carries on; however, the student behaviors have not changed, and there is no more direction from the teacher.

MESSAGE SENT:
There are no consequences for students who do not change behavior and therefore no expectation for change to occur.

ADMINISTRATION MIGHT ASK:
Is there a progression of consequences that extends beyond verbal redirection established for students repeatedly not following rules and procedures?

CONSTRUCTIVE FEEDBACK:
Establish and post a collaboratively created discipline progression chart in your class that defines the consequences students will encounter when rules and procedures are not followed—for example, verbal warning, conference with teacher, meeting with on-task buddy (could be a student or an adult), parent phone call, reflective time-out, behavioral contract, guidance referral, and discipline referral. This way the expectation for a change in behavior is encouraged,

and time is allowed for change to occur before administrative disciplinary action. Always be consistent and follow through on the consequences established. As student behavior changes, reinforce and encourage those behaviors through verbal and nonverbal cues, incentives, and so forth. Great discipline strategies also include establishing rules and procedures with students and posting those as well. Make every effort to make this process collaborative and encourage student ownership.

EXAMPLE-IN-PRACTICE SCENARIO:

During Mr. Jackson's class today, a group of students are very talkative. As Mr. Jackson provides specific praise to the groups who are on task, he reminds the off-task group, as a verbal warning, of the collaboratively created rules and procedures that they should be following. When the behavior does not change, he conferences with the group in private, reminding them again of the rules and procedures, and he has them explain how they can control their consequences. He makes sure that they take ownership of the upcoming consequence should the behavior not change. There are no more problems from the group, and Mr. Jackson makes sure to provide specific praise to encourage their continued engagement in on-task behaviors. The students are aware that Mr. Jackson follows through with the consequences set, never holds a grudge, and empowers the students by helping them to understand their choices. Therefore, he rarely gets to the end-of-the-class progression.

Message Sent is a practical guide that targets specific instructional strategies as feedback to teachers on practices observed during instruction through an administrative lens. As a resource to bridge the gap between teachers and administrators, this book aims to give educational teams a better understanding, through real-time scenarios and questioning, of the "message sent" during classroom observations. Undoubtedly, teachers will become more aware of their own instructional practices and opportunities for growth. Likewise, administrators will become more knowledgeable of the specific and actionable feedback needed in order to guide teachers in that growth.

About the Author

___

KAMILAH D. HOLDEN EARNED HER undergraduate degree from Bethune-Cookman University and her master of science degree in education from National University.

Holden has over a decade's worth of experience in the field of education, serving as a teacher, instructional coach, assistant principal, and principal in some of the largest districts in the United States. She has also worked in the Florida Department of Education, helping to support districts and school-based leadership teams develop systems for school improvement efforts.

Holden believes strongly in the importance of providing teachers with feedback that supports change and growth and realizes that not all administrators have enough experience with coaching or providing guidance to improve instruction. Message Sent represents her vision to support the efforts of both teachers and administrators.

REFERENCES

Cannon, M. D., & Witherspoon, R. (2005). Actionable feedback: Unlocking the power of learning and performance improvement. *The Academy of Management Executive (1993–2005)*, *19*(2), 120–134.

Cotton, K. (1989). School Improvement Research. Series III, 1988–89. Retrieved from http://files.eric.ed.gov/fulltext/ED312030.pdf

Cunningham, G. (2009). New Teacher's Companion: Practical Wisdom for Succeeding in the Classroom. Alexandria, VA, USA: Association for Supervision & Curriculum Development (ASCD). Retrieved from http://www.ebrary.com

DeZure, D., Kaplan, M., & Deerman, M. A. (2001). Research on student notetaking: Implications for faculty and graduate student instructors. CRLT Occasional Papers, 16. Retrieved from http://www.crlt.umich.edu/sites/default/files/resource_files/CRLT_no16.pdf

Fisher, D., & Frey, N. (2013). Better Learning Through Structured Teaching: A Framework for the Gradual Release of Responsibility. Alexandria, VA, USA: Association for Supervision & Curriculum Development (ASCD). Retrieved from http://www.ebrary.com

Hattie, J., & Timperley, H. (2007). "The power of feedback." *Review of Educational Research*, *77*(1), 81–112. DOI: 10.3102/003465430298487

Haynes, A. (2010). Lesson Planning and Preparation. London, GBR: Continuum International Publishing. Retrieved from http://www.ebrary.com

Jackson, R. R. (2009). Never Work Harder Than Your Students and Other Principles of Great Teaching. Alexandria, VA, USA: Association for

Supervision & Curriculum Development (ASCD). Retrieved from http://www.ebrary.com

Jackson, R. R. (2011). How to Plan Rigorous Instruction (Mastering the Principles of Great Teaching). Alexandria, VA, USA: Association for Supervision & Curriculum Development (ASCD). Retrieved from http://www.ebrary.com

James-Ward, C., Fisher, D., & Frey, N. (2013). Using Data to Focus Instructional Improvement. Alexandria, VA, USA: Association for Supervision & Curriculum Development (ASCD). Retrieved from http://www.ebrary.com

Kunter, M., Baumert, J., & Köller, O. (2007). Effective classroom management and the development of subject-related interest. *Learning and Instruction, 17*(5), 494–509. doi:10.1016/j.learninstruc.2007.09.002

Martella, R. C., Nelson, J. R., & Marchand-Martella, N. E. (2011). Comprehensive Behavior Management: Individualized, Classroom, and Schoolwide Approaches (2nd Edition). Thousand Oaks, CA, USA: SAGE Publications, Inc. Retrieved from http://www.ebrary.com

Marzano, R. J., Gaddy, B. B., & Foseid, M. C. (2005). Handbook for Classroom Management That Works. Alexandria, VA, USA: Association for Supervision & Curriculum Development (ASCD). Retrieved from http://www.ebrary.com

McLeod, J., Fisher, J., & Hoover, G. (2003). Key Elements of Classroom Management: Managing Time and Space, Student Behavior, and Instructional Strategies. Alexandria, VA, USA: Association for Supervision & Curriculum Development (ASCD). Retrieved from http://www.ebrary.com

Slavin, R. E. (2014). *Making cooperative learning powerful*. Alexandria, VA, USA: Association for Supervision & Curriculum Development (ASCD). Retrieved from http://www.ebrary.com

Stronge, J. H., Tucker, P. D., & Hindman, J. L. (2004). Handbook for Qualities of Effective Teachers. Alexandria, VA, USA: Association for Supervision & Curriculum Development (ASCD). Retrieved from http://www.ebrary.com

Stuhlman, M. W., Hamre, B. K., Downer, J. T., & Pianta, R. C. (n.d.). A Practitioner's Guide to Conducting Classroom Observations: What the Research Tells Us About Choosing and Using Observational Systems to Assess and Improve Teacher Effectiveness. *Why Should We Use Classroom Observation?* Retrieved from http://curry.virginia.edu/uploads/resourceLibrary/CASTL_practioner_Part1_single.pdf

Tomlinson, C. A. (2014). *The differentiated classroom: Responding to the needs of all learners* (2nd Edition). Alexandria, VA, USA: Association for Supervision & Curriculum Development (ASCD). Retrieved from http://www.ebrary.com

Waldman, C., & Crippen, K. J. (2009). Integrating interactive notebooks. *The Science Teacher, 76*(1), 51–55. Retrieved from http://www.gcisd-k12.org/cms/lib4/TX01000829/Centricity/Domain/75/interactivenotebooks.pdf

Willis, J. (2006). Research-Based Strategies to Ignite Student Learning: Insights from a Neurologist and Classroom Teacher. Alexandria, VA, USA: Association for Supervision & Curriculum Development (ASCD). Retrieved from http://www.ebrary.com

Wong, H., & Wong, R. (2000). Effective Teaching: How to start a class effectively. Teachers.net gazette, 3(10). Retrieved from http://www.teachers.net/wong/OCT00/wongprint.html

Wong, H., Wong, R., Rogers, K., & Brooks, A. (2012). Managing your classroom for success. *Science and Children, 49*(10), 60–64. Retrieved from http://tccl.rit.albany.edu/knilt/images/3/30/Classroom_Management_Success_Wong_et_al.pdf

Made in the USA
Coppell, TX
19 March 2022